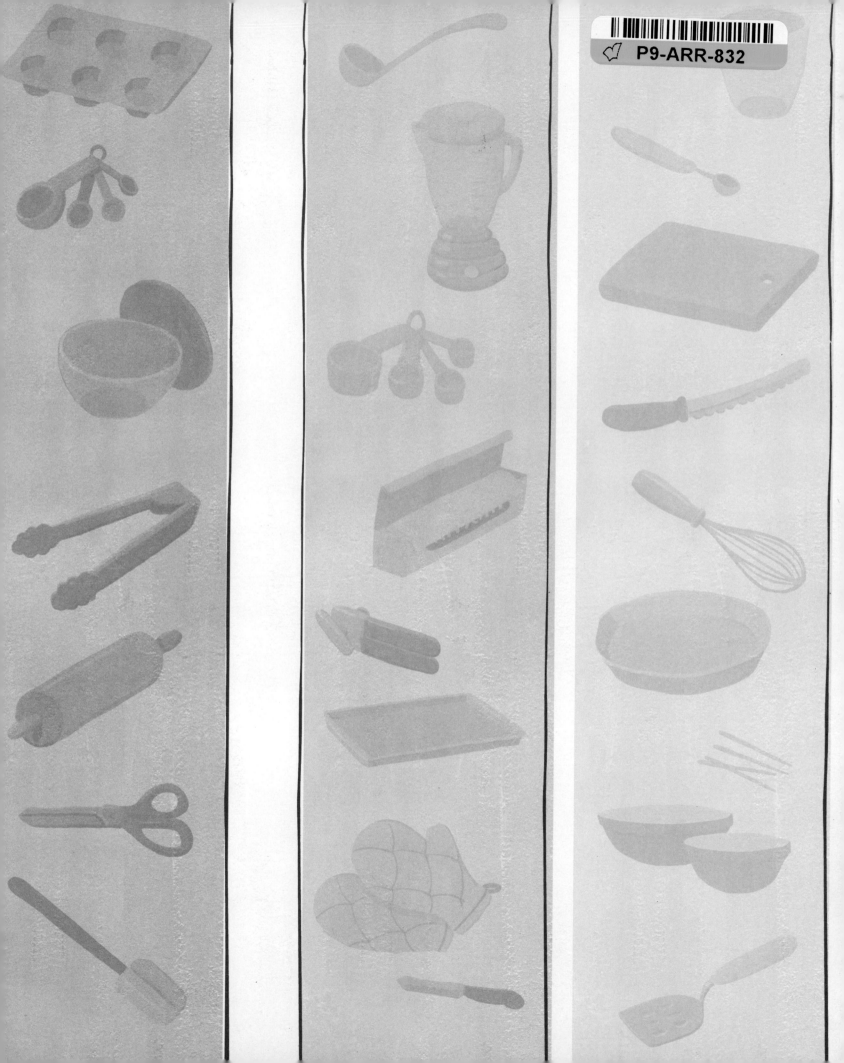

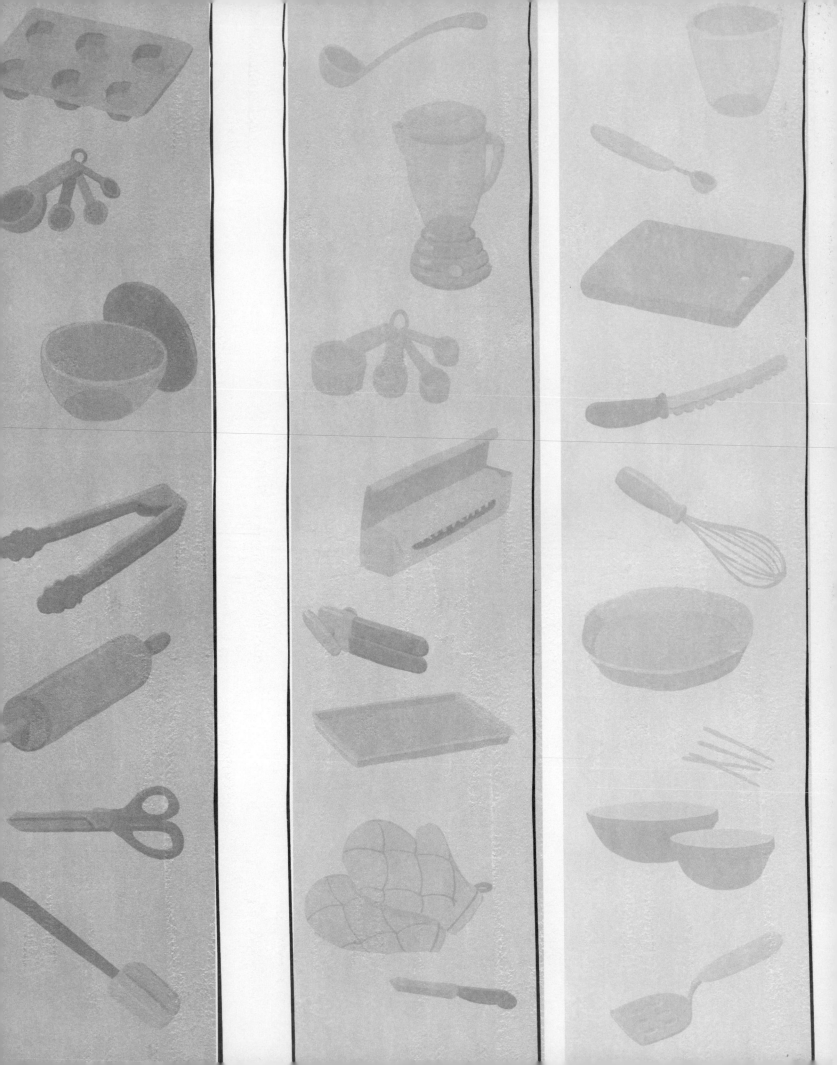

Holy Guacamole!

and Other Scrumptious Snacks

by Nick Fauchald   illustrated by Rick Peterson

Special thanks to our content adviser:
Joanne L. Slavin, Ph.D., R.D.
Professor of Food Science and Nutrition
University of Minnesota

PICTURE WINDOW BOOKS
Minneapolis, Minnesota

Editors: Christianne Jones and Carol Jones
Designer: Tracy Davies
Page Production: Melissa Kes

Art Director: Nathan Gassman
The illustrations in this book were created with acrylics and gouache.

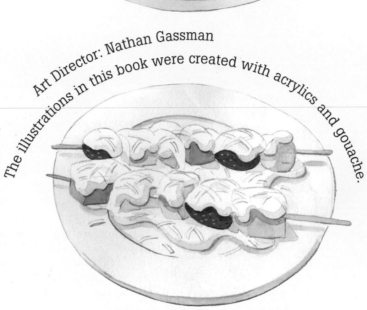

The illustration on page 5 is from *www.mypyramid.gov*.

Printed in the United States of America
 All books published by Picture Window Books are manufactured
with paper containing at least 10 percent post-consumer waste.

Library of Congress Cataloging-in-Publication Data
Fauchald, Nick.
Holy guacamole! : and other scrumptious snacks / by Nick Fauchald ; illustrated by Rick Peterson.
p. cm. — (Kids dish)
Includes index.
ISBN-13: 978-1-4048-3995-3 (library binding)
1. Snack foods—Juvenile literature. 2. Cookery—Juvenile literature. I. Peterson, Rick. II. Title.
TX740.F375 2008
641.5'3—dc22   2007032929

Editors' note: The author based the difficulty levels of the recipes on the skills and time required, as well
as the number of ingredients and tools needed. Adult help and supervision is required for all recipes.

Table of Contents

EASY

INTERMEDIATE

ADVANCED

Nick Fauchald is the author of many children's books. After attending the French Culinary School in Manhattan, he helped launch the magazine *Every Day with Rachael Ray*. He is currently an editor at *Food & Wine* magazine and lives in New York City. Although Nick has worked with some of the world's best chefs, he still thinks kids are the most fun and creative cooks to work with.

Dear Kids,

Healthy snacks are a key part of your diet. They give you the energy to stay active between meals. This cookbook is packed with delicious and healthy snack recipes. Plus, they're are easy enough to make with only a little help from an adult.

Cooking is fun, and safety in the kitchen is very important. As you begin your cooking adventure, please remember these tips:

★ Make sure an adult is in the kitchen with you.
★ Tie back your hair and tuck in all loose clothing.
★ Read the recipe from start to finish before you begin.
★ Wash your hands before you start and whenever they get messy.
★ Wash all fresh fruits and vegetables.
★ Take your time cutting the ingredients.
★ Use oven mitts whenever you are working with hot foods or equipment.
★ Stay in the kitchen the entire time you are cooking.
★ Clean up when you are finished.

Now, choose a recipe that sounds tasty, check with an adult, and get cooking. Your friends and family are hungry!

Enjoy,
Nick

Note to Adults:

Learning to cook is an exciting, challenging adventure for young people. It helps kids build confidence, learn responsibility, become familiar with food and nutrition, practice math, science, and motor skills, and follow directions. Here are some ways you can help kids get the most out of their cooking experiences:

• Encourage them to read the entire recipe before they begin cooking. Make sure they have everything they need and understand all of the steps.

• Make sure young cooks have a kid-friendly workspace. If your kitchen counter is too high for them, offer them a stepstool or a table to work at.

• Expect new cooks to make a little mess, and encourage them to clean it up when they are finished.

• Help multiple cooks divide the tasks before they begin.

• Enjoy what the kids just cooked together.

MyPyramid

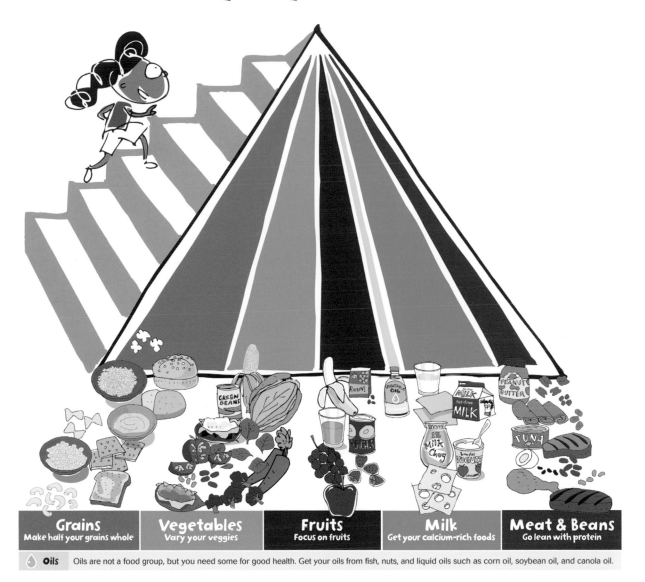

Grains Make half your grains whole	**Vegetables** Vary your veggies	**Fruits** Focus on fruits	**Milk** Get your calcium-rich foods	**Meat & Beans** Go lean with protein

💧 **Oils** Oils are not a food group, but you need some for good health. Get your oils from fish, nuts, and liquid oils such as corn oil, soybean oil, and canola oil.

In 2005, the U.S. government created MyPyramid, a plan for healthy eating and living. The new MyPyramid plan contains 12 separate diet plans based on your age, gender, and activity level. For more information about MyPyramid, visit *www.mypyramid.gov*.

The pyramid at the top of each recipe shows the main food groups included. Use the index to find recipes that include food from the food group of your choice, major ingredients used, recipe levels, and appliances/equipment needed.

Special Tips and Glossary

Cracking Eggs: Tap the egg on the counter until it cracks. Hold the egg over a small bowl. Gently pull the two halves of the shell apart until the contents fall into the bowl.

Measuring Dry Ingredients: Measure dry ingredients (such as flour and sugar) by spooning the ingredient into a measuring cup until it's full. Then level off the top of the cup with the back of a butter knife.

Measuring Wet Ingredients: Place a clear measuring cup on a flat surface, then pour the liquid into the cup until it reaches the correct measuring line. Be sure to check the liquid at eye level.

Bake: cook food in an oven

Brush: spread a liquid or sauce with a pastry brush

Cool: set hot food on a wire rack until it's no longer hot

Cover: put container lid, plastic wrap, or aluminum foil over a food; use aluminum foil if you're baking the food, and plastic wrap if you're chilling, freezing, microwaving, or leaving it on the counter

Drain: pour off a liquid, leaving food behind; usually done with a strainer or colander

Drizzle: to lightly pour

Grease: spread butter, cooking spray, or shortening on a piece of cookware so food doesn't stick

Melt: heat a solid (such as butter) until it becomes a liquid

Peel: remove the skin from a fruit or vegetable; be careful—peelers are sharp!

Preheat: turn an oven on before you use it; it usually takes about 15 minutes to preheat an oven

Slice: cut something into thin pieces

Spread: to make an even layer of something soft, like mayonnaise or frosting

Sprinkle: to scatter something in small bits

Stir: mix ingredients with a spoon until blended

Whisk: stir a mixture rapidly until it's smooth

METRIC CONVERSION CHART

1/8 teaspoon (0.5 milliliter)
1/4 teaspoon (1 milliliter)
1/2 teaspoon (2.5 milliliters)
1 teaspoon (5 milliliters)
2 teaspoons (10 milliliters)

1 tablespoon (15 milliliters)
2 tablespoons (30 milliliters)
3 tablespoons (45 milliliters)

1/4 cup (60 milliliters)
1/2 cup (125 milliliters)
2/3 cup (150 milliliters)
3/4 cup (180 milliliters)
1 cup (250 milliliters)
2 cups (500 milliliters)

8 ounces (227 grams)
9 ounces (255 grams)
12 ounces (355 grams)
15 ounces (425 grams)

TEMPERATURE CONVERSION CHART

350° Fahrenheit (175° Celsius)
375° Fahrenheit (190° Celsius)
425° Fahrenheit (220° Celsius)

Kitchen Tools

HERE ARE THE TOOLS YOU'LL USE WHEN COOKING THE RECIPES IN THIS BOOK★

8-by-8-inch baking pan

Baking sheet

Blender

Butter knife

Can opener

Cooking spray

Cutting board

Drinking glass

Fork

Kitchen shears

Liquid measuring cup

Measuring cups

Measuring spoons

Mesh strainer

Melon baller

Microwave-safe bowls

Oven mitts

Paper cups

Paper towels

Pastry brush

Plastic bags

Plate

Plastic wrap

Popsicle sticks

Rubber spatula

Mixing bowls

Serrated knife

Spoon

Small, sharp knife

Wooden skewers

Wooden spoon

Whisk

Vegetable peeler

7

This Recipe Includes
FRUITS, MILK

Pineapple Popsicles

INGREDIENTS

1/2 cup canned,
    crushed pineapple
2 cups plain low-fat yogurt
12-ounce can frozen orange
    juice concentrate, thawed

TOOLS

Mesh strainer
2 medium mixing bowls
Can opener
Measuring cups
Wooden spoon
4 paper cups, 9 ounces each
Plastic wrap
4 wooden Popsicle sticks or
    plastic spoons

1 Place the mesh strainer over a medium mixing bowl. Open the can of pineapple. Pour the pineapple into the strainer and let the juice drain.

2 Put the yogurt, drained pineapple, and orange juice concentrate into another medium mixing bowl and stir.

3 Spoon the mixture into the paper cups, filling them almost to the top. Stretch a small piece of plastic wrap across the top of each cup.

4 Poke the wooden sticks or plastic spoons through the plastic wrap and into the fruit mixture. Stand the sticks straight up in the center of the cups.

5 Place the cups on a level surface in the freezer for 6 hours or until the mixture is frozen solid. Remove from the freezer.

6 Remove the plastic wrap, peel away the paper cup, and serve.

This Recipe Includes
VEGETABLES, MILK

Pimiento Cheese Dip

INGREDIENTS

1 cup jarred pimientos, drained
1 cup chive and onion cream cheese
1/4 cup plain low-fat yogurt
8-ounce bag shredded cheddar cheese
1/8 teaspoon salt
Assorted dippers, such as celery sticks and pretzel rods (1 cup per person)

TOOLS

Measuring cups
Spoon
Paper towels
Cutting board
Small knife
Rubber spatula
Large mixing bowl
Fork
Measuring spoons
Wooden spoon

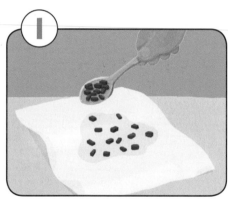
Spoon the pimientos onto a paper towel to drain. Wash the celery and ask an adult to cut it.

Use a rubber spatula to scoop the cream cheese into a large mixing bowl. With a fork, mash and stir the cream cheese until it's soft and fluffy.

Add the yogurt and stir with a fork.

Add the cheddar, salt, and pimientos. Stir.

5 Serve with the celery sticks and pretzel rods.

MEAT & BEANS,
GRAINS, DAIRY

Quesadilla Bites

INGREDIENTS
9-ounce bag tortilla chips
15-ounce can refried beans
1/2 cup salsa
1 cup shredded taco cheese

TOOLS
Large plate
Can opener
Measuring spoons
Measuring cups

Spread 12 tortilla chips on a large plate.

Open the can of refried beans. Place a heaping teaspoon of refried beans on each chip.

Top the beans with 2 teaspoons of salsa.

Sprinkle cheese over the salsa.

5

Cover the cheese with another chip to make 12 mini quesadillas.

6 Serve.

This Recipe Includes
GRAINS, FRUITS

Quick Energy Trail Mix

INGREDIENTS
1/2 cup pretzel sticks
1/2 cup dried apricots
1/2 cup raisins
1/4 cup dried cranberries
1/2 cup whole-wheat
   squares cereal
1/2 cup granola
1/4 cup sunflower seeds
1/2 cup unsalted peanuts,
   almonds, or cashews,
   optional

TOOLS
Measuring cups
Large mixing bowl
Kitchen shears
Cutting board
Quart-size plastic bags,
   optional

NUTRITION NOTE★
Almonds are rich in
magnesium, which is
important for building
strong bones and keeping
your heart healthy.

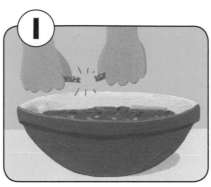

1 Break the pretzel sticks in half and place them into a large mixing bowl.

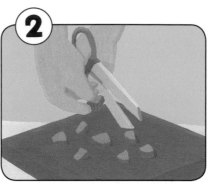

2 Cut the apricots into pieces with the kitchen shears and add them to the pretzels.

3 Add the rest of the ingredients and mix with your hands.

4 Serve right away or pack in four quart-size bags for later.

14

Citrusy Soda Pop

1

Place the orange juice concentrate into the measuring cup. Add the lemon and lime juices and stir.

2

Fill four glasses with ice cubes. Pour the juice mixture into the glasses.

3 Top each glass with the seltzer water, stir, and serve.

INGREDIENTS

3/4 cup frozen orange juice concentrate, thawed

3 tablespoons fresh lemon juice

3 tablespoons fresh lime juice

12 to 16 ice cubes

1 cup seltzer water

TOOLS

4-cup liquid measuring cup

Measuring spoons

Spoon

4 drinking glasses

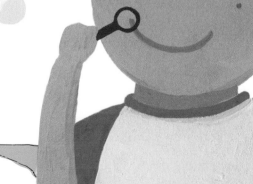

NUTRITION NOTE★ Orange juice is high in vitamin C, which helps your body fight illness.

This Recipe Includes
GRAINS, FRUITS, MEAT & BEANS

Mini Pepperoni Pizzas

INGREDIENTS
2 English muffins
1 medium tomato
1/2 cup pizza sauce
16 slices pepperoni
1/2 cup shredded
    mozzarella cheese

TOOLS
Serrated knife
Baking sheet
Cutting board
Measuring cups
Measuring spoons
Oven mitts

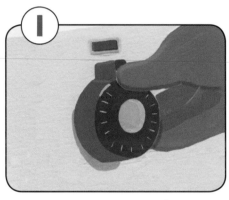

Preheat the oven to 375°.

Split the English muffins in half and place them on a baking sheet.

Ask an adult to cut the tomato crosswise into 1/8-inch slices.

Layer each half of the English muffin with 1 1/2 tablespoons of pizza sauce, 4 slices of pepperoni, and 2 tablespoons of cheese.

NUTRITION NOTE★ Tomatoes are often considered vegetables, but they are the fruits of the tomato plant.

5

Top each muffin half with one slice of tomato.

6

Ask an adult to bake the pizzas for 12 minutes or until the cheese is melted and the muffins are crispy. Let cool for 5 minutes.

7 Place pizzas on plate and serve.

This Recipe Includes
GRAINS

Spicy Tortilla Chips

INGREDIENTS

8 corn tortillas, plain or
    assorted colors
1/4 teaspoon cumin
1/4 teaspoon chili powder
2 teaspoons kosher salt
Salsa for serving, optional

TOOLS

2 baking sheets
Cooking spray
Kitchen shears
Measuring spoons
Small mixing bowl
Oven mitts

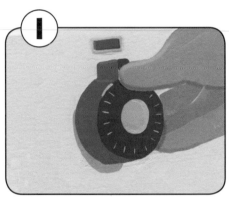

Preheat the oven to 375°.

Grease two baking sheets with
cooking spray.

Make a stack of two tortillas. With
the kitchen shears, cut the tortillas
into wedges and place the wedges
on the baking sheets. Repeat with
the remaining tortillas.

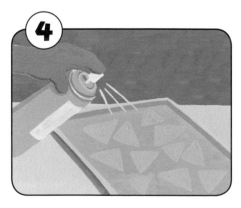

Lightly spray the tortillas with
cooking spray.

18

5

In a small mixing bowl, stir the cumin, chili powder, and salt. Lightly sprinkle the salt mixture on top of the tortilla wedges.

6

Ask an adult to bake the tortillas for 12 minutes or until crispy. Let cool for 10 minutes.

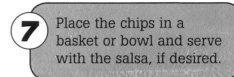

7 Place the chips in a basket or bowl and serve with the salsa, if desired.

This Recipe Includes

FRUITS, MILK

Monkey Milkshakes

INGREDIENTS
1 banana
3 tablespoons creamy
    peanut butter
2/3 cup chocolate milk
6 to 8 ice cubes

TOOLS
Butter knife
Cutting board
Measuring spoons
Measuring cups
Blender
2 drinking glasses

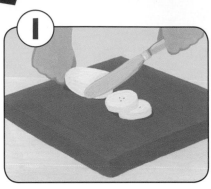

1 Peel the banana and cut it into slices.

2 Place the banana slices, peanut butter, and chocolate milk into a blender. Cover and blend for 15 seconds or until smooth.

3 Add the ice cubes. Cover and blend again for 30 seconds or until smooth.

4 Pour into drinking glasses and serve.

NUTRITION NOTE★
Peanut butter is rich in protein, which is important for building strong bones and muscles.

Chili Cheese Popcorn

1 Ask an adult to cook the popcorn in the microwave according to package directions. Pour the popcorn into a large mixing bowl.

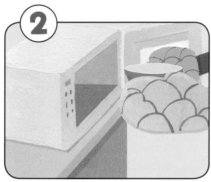

2 Place the butter in a small microwave-safe bowl. Ask an adult to heat the butter in the microwave for 30 seconds or until melted.

3 Add the chili powder and garlic powder to the butter and stir.

4 Drizzle the butter mixture over the popcorn and stir to coat.

5 Sprinkle the popcorn with Parmesan cheese and salt and serve.

INGREDIENTS

1 bag of plain
   microwave popcorn
2 tablespoons butter
1 teaspoon chili powder
1/8 teaspoon garlic powder
2 tablespoons freshly grated
   Parmesan cheese
1/4 teaspoon salt

TOOLS

Large mixing bowl
Measuring spoons
Small microwave-safe bowl
Oven mitts
Wooden spoon

This Recipe Includes

FRUITS

Raisiny Applesauce

INGREDIENTS
4 apples
3 tablespoons fresh
   lemon juice
2 teaspoons sugar
1/2 cup apple juice
1/4 teaspoon cinnamon
1/4 cup raisins

TOOLS
Vegetable peeler
Serrated knife
Cutting board
Melon baller
Measuring spoons
Measuring cups
Blender
Medium bowl
Spoon

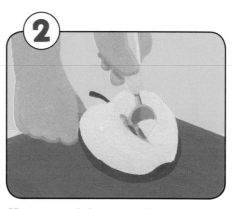

Wash the apples and remove the peel with the vegetable peeler.

Have an adult cut each apple in half. Use a melon baller to remove the core and seeds.

Ask an adult to cut each apple half into eight large chunks.

Place the apples, lemon juice, sugar, apple juice, and cinnamon into the blender. Cover and blend for 15 seconds or until smooth.

22

FOOD FACT★ When an apple is cut, the pieces turn brown. To keep your apple fresh, rub the apple pieces with lemon juice.

5 Pour the applesauce into a medium bowl.

6 Add the raisins, stir, and serve.

This Recipe Includes

FRUITS, MILK

Yogurt Fruit Kabobs

INGREDIENTS

1 cup plain low-fat yogurt

2 tablespoons pure maple syrup

2 cups assorted washed and cut-up fruit, such as bananas, pineapples, apples, oranges, and strawberries

1/2 cup shredded coconut, optional

TOOLS

Measuring cups

Measuring spoons

Medium mixing bowl

Spoon

2 plates

4 wooden skewers

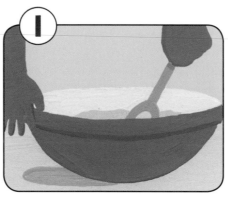

1 Pour the yogurt and the maple syrup into a mixing bowl and stir.

2 Pour the yogurt mixture onto a plate.

3 If using, spread the coconut on another plate.

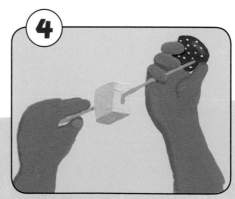

4 Place the fruit on the skewers, alternating the fruit any way you like.

5

Roll a fruit kabob in the yogurt, using a spoon to help cover the fruit with yogurt.

6

If desired, roll the yogurt-covered kabobs in the coconut, using your fingers to sprinkle some of the coconut over the fruit. Place the kabob on a plate.

7 Repeat with the remaining kabobs and serve.

This Recipe Includes
GRAINS, MEAT & BEANS

Parmesan Pita Chips

INGREDIENTS
4 whole wheat pita
   bread rounds
1/4 cup extra-virgin
   olive oil
1/2 cup freshly grated
   Parmesan cheese
1 cup hummus, for dipping

TOOLS
Kitchen shears
Baking sheet
Measuring cups
Pastry brush
Oven mitts

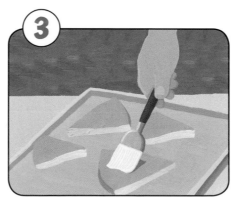

Preheat the oven to 425°.

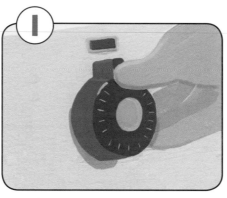

Using a kitchen shears, cut each pita bread in half and cut each half into four wedges. Place the pita wedges onto a baking sheet.

Brush each pita wedge with olive oil.

Sprinkle the Parmesan cheese on top of the wedges.

26

NUTRITION NOTE★ Whole wheat bread is a great source of complex carbohydrates, which your body uses for fuel.

5 Ask an adult to bake the pita wedges for 7 minutes or until they are lightly browned and crispy. Let cool.

6 Pour the pita chips into a bowl and serve with the hummus.

This Recipe Includes
FRUITS, GRAINS

Gooey Granola Bars

INGREDIENTS

1 egg
1/2 cup brown sugar
1 teaspoon vanilla extract
1 cup granola
1/2 cup raisins or dried
  cranberries
3 tablespoons semi-sweet
  chocolate chips
1/2 cup chopped peanuts
  or almonds, optional

TOOLS

8-by-8-inch baking pan
Cooking spray
Medium mixing bowl
Measuring cups
Measuring spoons
Whisk
Wooden spoon
Oven mitts
Small knife

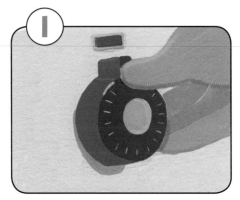

Preheat the oven to 350°.

Grease the baking pan with cooking spray.

Crack the egg into a medium mixing bowl.

Add the brown sugar and vanilla extract to the egg and whisk until combined.

NUTRITION NOTE★ Nuts are a good source of omega-3 fatty acids—the type of fat that helps fight disease.

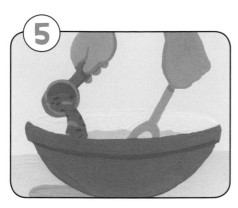

Add the granola, raisins, chocolate chips, and nuts. Stir.

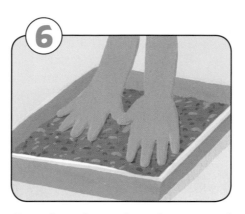

Pour the mixture into the pan and spread evenly over the bottom, pressing firmly with your hands.

Ask an adult to bake the granola bars for 25 minutes or until golden brown. Let cool in the pan for 1 hour.

8 Cut into nine bars and serve.

This Recipe Includes **GRAINS, FRUITS**

Holy Guacamole!

INGREDIENTS
2 ripe avocados
3 tablespoons fresh
   lime juice
1/2 teaspoon cumin
1/4 teaspoon salt
1 tablespoon salsa
3 sprigs cilantro
9-ounce bag of tortilla
   chips, for serving

TOOLS
Serrated knife
Cutting board
Spoon
Medium mixing bowl
Fork
Measuring spoons
Kitchen shears

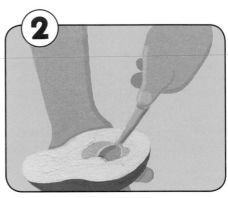

1. Ask an adult to cut an avocado in half lengthwise. Twist the two avocado halves to separate them. Remove the pits and discard. Repeat with the remaining avocado.

2. Scoop out the avocado insides with a spoon and place them in a medium mixing bowl.

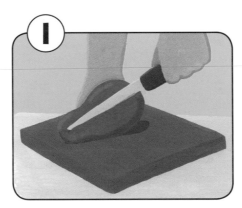

3. Mash the avocados with a fork.

4. Add the lime juice, cumin, salt, and salsa and stir.

NUTRITION NOTE★ An avocado is a fruit that is high in potassium, which helps maintain a healthy nervous system.

5 With the shears, snip the cilantro into small pieces and stir into the guacamole.

6 Serve with tortilla chips.

INDEX

ON THE WEB

FactHound offers a safe, fun way to find Web sites related to topics in this book. All of the sites on FactHound have been researched by our staff.

1.   Visit *www.facthound.com*
2.   Type in this special code: 140483995X
3.   Click on the FETCH IT button.

Your trusty FactHound will fetch the best sites for you!

KIDS DISH

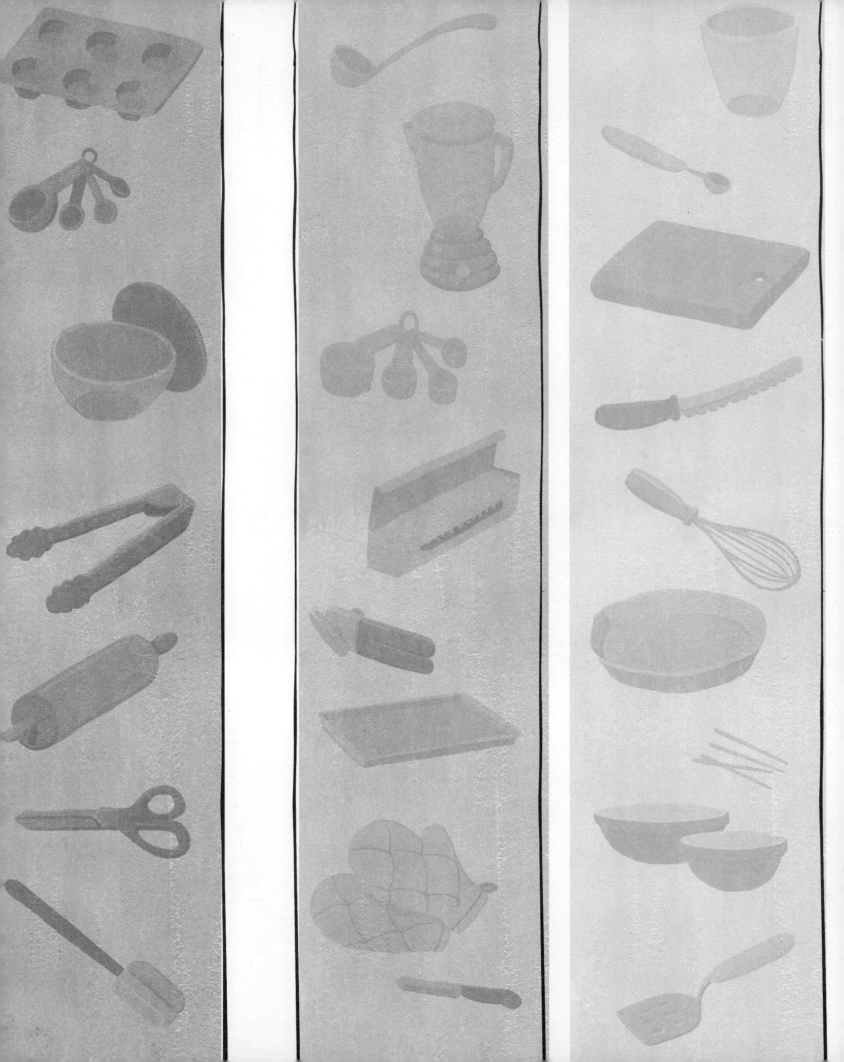

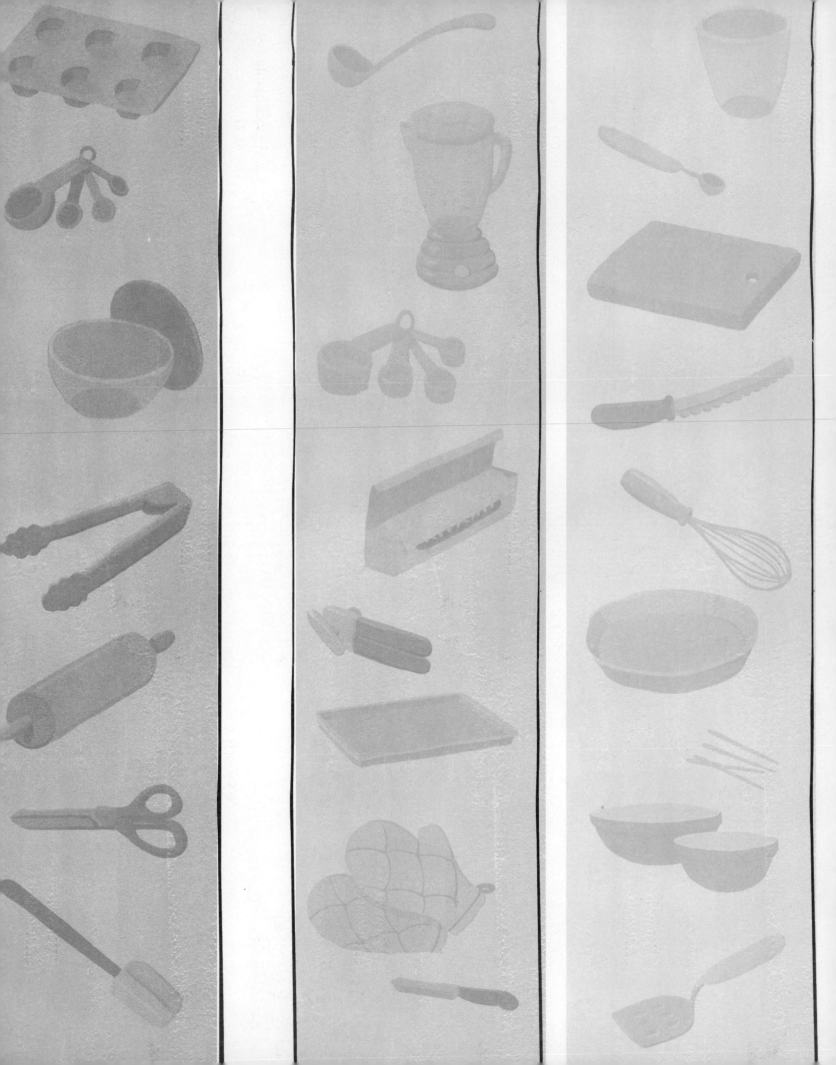